The Gumdrop Tree

by Elizabeth Markert Rizza

illustrated by Mig Sertl

To order additional copies of this book, contact:
Xlibris
1-888-795-4274
www.Xlibris.com
Orders@Xlibris.com

Book Designer: Jonah Goodman

ISBN: Softcover   978-1-4010-9558-1
        Hardcover   978-1-4257-1141-2

Library of Congress Control Number: 2003090859

Print information available on the last page

Rev. date: 11/23/2019

A Note to Parents

Please remind your children **never** to eat anything they see growing in the wild. Berry picking is an activity which must always be supervised by an adult.

To my father
who taught me to believe

and in memory of my Uncle Dave
for a great beginning

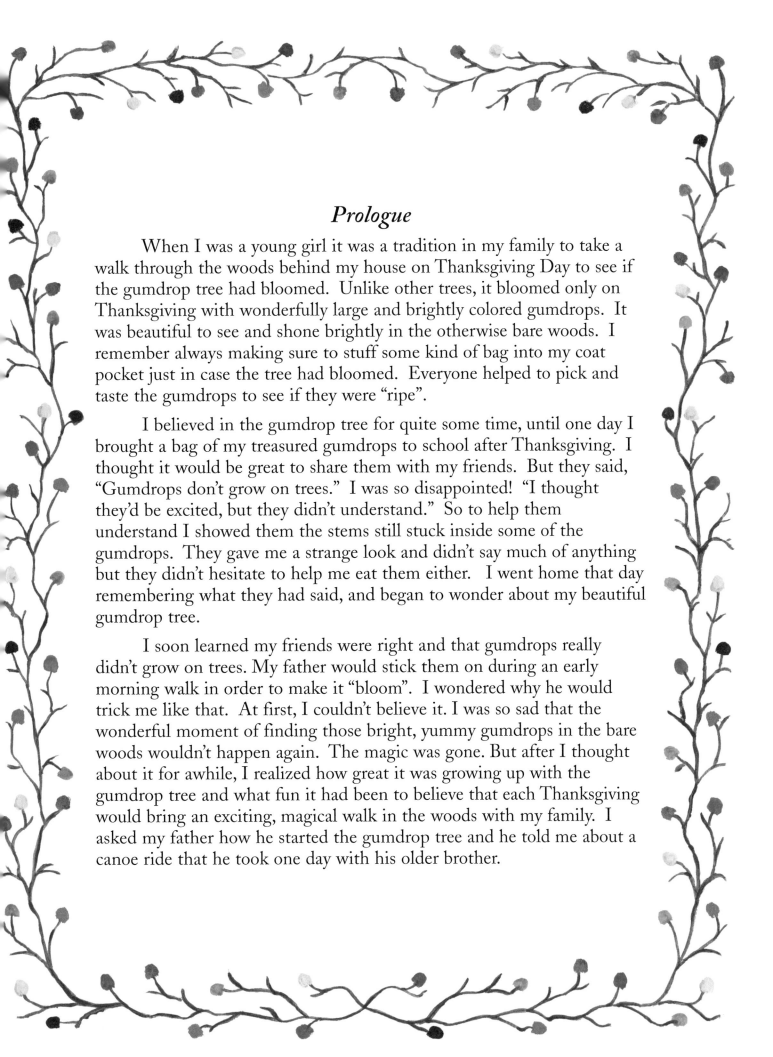

Prologue

When I was a young girl it was a tradition in my family to take a walk through the woods behind my house on Thanksgiving Day to see if the gumdrop tree had bloomed. Unlike other trees, it bloomed only on Thanksgiving with wonderfully large and brightly colored gumdrops. It was beautiful to see and shone brightly in the otherwise bare woods. I remember always making sure to stuff some kind of bag into my coat pocket just in case the tree had bloomed. Everyone helped to pick and taste the gumdrops to see if they were "ripe".

I believed in the gumdrop tree for quite some time, until one day I brought a bag of my treasured gumdrops to school after Thanksgiving. I thought it would be great to share them with my friends. But they said, "Gumdrops don't grow on trees." I was so disappointed! "I thought they'd be excited, but they didn't understand." So to help them understand I showed them the stems still stuck inside some of the gumdrops. They gave me a strange look and didn't say much of anything but they didn't hesitate to help me eat them either. I went home that day remembering what they had said, and began to wonder about my beautiful gumdrop tree.

I soon learned my friends were right and that gumdrops really didn't grow on trees. My father would stick them on during an early morning walk in order to make it "bloom". I wondered why he would trick me like that. At first, I couldn't believe it. I was so sad that the wonderful moment of finding those bright, yummy gumdrops in the bare woods wouldn't happen again. The magic was gone. But after I thought about it for awhile, I realized how great it was growing up with the gumdrop tree and what fun it had been to believe that each Thanksgiving would bring an exciting, magical walk in the woods with my family. I asked my father how he started the gumdrop tree and he told me about a canoe ride that he took one day with his older brother.

Towards the end of a beautiful fall day two brothers went for a canoe ride. The older brother, David, sat in the front and little Robert in the back. As they slid through the water, colored leaves floating by were sometimes pulled under water by the tiny whirlpools flowing from their paddles. Puffy white clouds in the clear blue sky were reflected in the smooth, calm surface of the lake.

They had paddled for a long time and Robert was getting very tired. The sun would be setting soon and David decided they should head for home before his little brother became too tired to paddle. They slowly followed the shoreline towards home.

Brushing by the wild blueberry bushes, Robert wondered how long it would be until next summer when the leaves were on the trees and the bushes were in bloom again, heavy with the tiny, but sweet, berries.

Dragging his paddle in the water, Robert began to daydream about picking blueberries. David saw that his brother was tired so he reached into his pocket, and pulled out a few gumdrops he had been saving for the trip. He was going to offer one to Robert but a bright red one caught his eye and he thought of a game to help make the paddling seem easier. As they passed another bush he quickly stuck the gumdrop on the pointed end of a twig. His little brother hadn't noticed what he had done. He was too busy daydreaming about next summer's harvest of blueberries.

As the boat slipped by the bush it brought little Robert right to the bright red gumdrop. At first Robert thought he was seeing a wild berry bush, but remembered that it was fall and all the berries were gone. What kind of bush would bloom in the fall he wondered? Then a little further on there was another one! This time it was yellow. Robert looked closely at it.

"Wow! Those berries look a lot like gumdrops", he thought. "Wait", he shouted to his big brother. "I see gumdrops!"

"Gumdrops?" said his brother doubtfully. "Gumdrops don't grow on trees."

Robert insisted. "I *know* they're gumdrops. I just know they are! Can't we stop to see?"

"Well, I guess it couldn't hurt to look," said David as he smiled.

So they paddled back to where little Robert had seen the last one. As the bright yellow gumdrop came into sight Robert shouted excitedly, "I knew it! You see! It *is* a gumdrop!"

Robert's brother looked over the berry very carefully. Then he tasted a little piece of it pretending that he hadn't seen it before and that he was making sure it wasn't poisonous. When he had decided that it was all right to eat, he broke off a piece and gave it to Robert who popped his treasure in his mouth. First, he sucked the sugar off and then savored the lemony flavor. Finally, he gave it one last chomp and swallowed the rest.

With the taste of lemon still in his mouth, Robert wondered if there were more gumdrops to be found. "Let's paddle a little further and see if we can find some more!"

"Oh, I wouldn't get your hopes up," said David. "There are probably very few of them left. Someone else may have found them before us."

Robert thought for a minute. Then he said, "Maybe *we* are the first people to find them. If someone else *had* been here they probably wouldn't have left any behind."

"Yeah, you're probably right," David said sarcastically. "When people find something very rare they usually get scared that they'll never have a chance to get anymore, so they take every last bit for themselves".

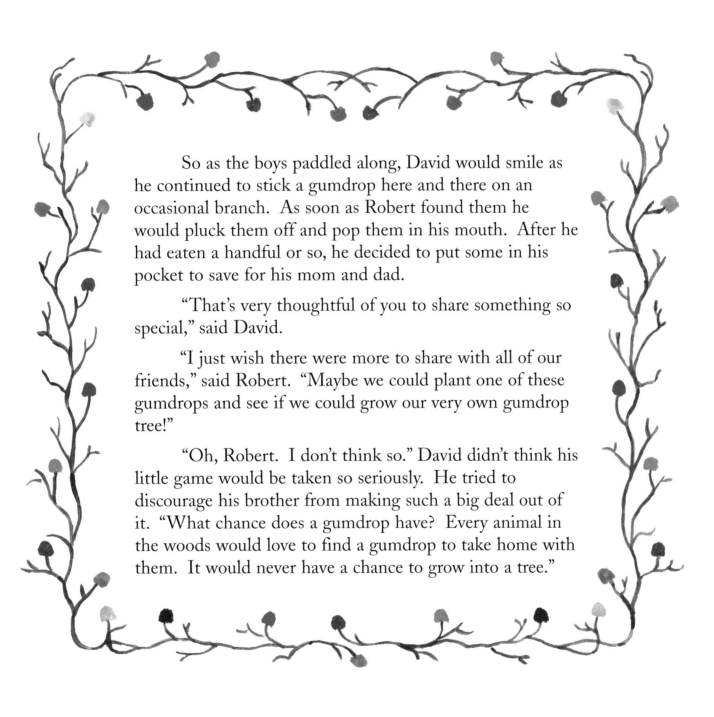

So as the boys paddled along, David would smile as he continued to stick a gumdrop here and there on an occasional branch. As soon as Robert found them he would pluck them off and pop them in his mouth. After he had eaten a handful or so, he decided to put some in his pocket to save for his mom and dad.

"That's very thoughtful of you to share something so special," said David.

"I just wish there were more to share with all of our friends," said Robert. "Maybe we could plant one of these gumdrops and see if we could grow our very own gumdrop tree!"

"Oh, Robert. I don't think so." David didn't think his little game would be taken so seriously. He tried to discourage his brother from making such a big deal out of it. "What chance does a gumdrop have? Every animal in the woods would love to find a gumdrop to take home with them. It would never have a chance to grow into a tree."

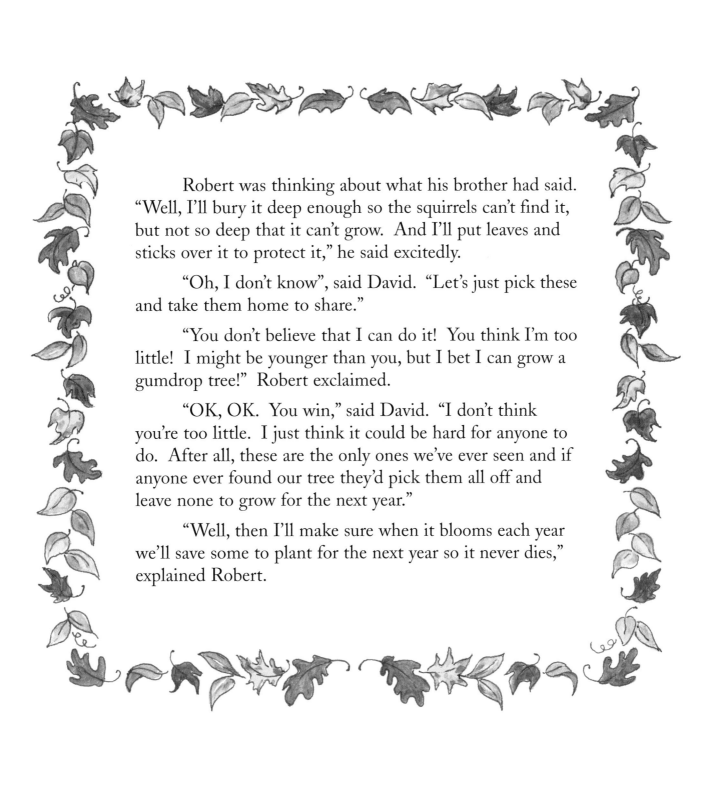

Robert was thinking about what his brother had said. "Well, I'll bury it deep enough so the squirrels can't find it, but not so deep that it can't grow. And I'll put leaves and sticks over it to protect it," he said excitedly.

"Oh, I don't know", said David. "Let's just pick these and take them home to share."

"You don't believe that I can do it! You think I'm too little! I might be younger than you, but I bet I can grow a gumdrop tree!" Robert exclaimed.

"OK, OK. You win," said David. "I don't think you're too little. I just think it could be hard for anyone to do. After all, these are the only ones we've ever seen and if anyone ever found our tree they'd pick them all off and leave none to grow for the next year."

"Well, then I'll make sure when it blooms each year we'll save some to plant for the next year so it never dies," explained Robert.

David smiled to himself. The idea of a gumdrop tree blooming every year, especially around Thanksgiving, could be a lot of fun. But he was also concerned that his little brother might become disappointed believing in something that was just make-believe. Well, he'd worry about that later. Right now they had to get home because it was really getting dark and their parents would be getting concerned. As soon as they docked the canoe, Robert ran up the steps to his house to show his parents the wonderful gumdrops he had found.

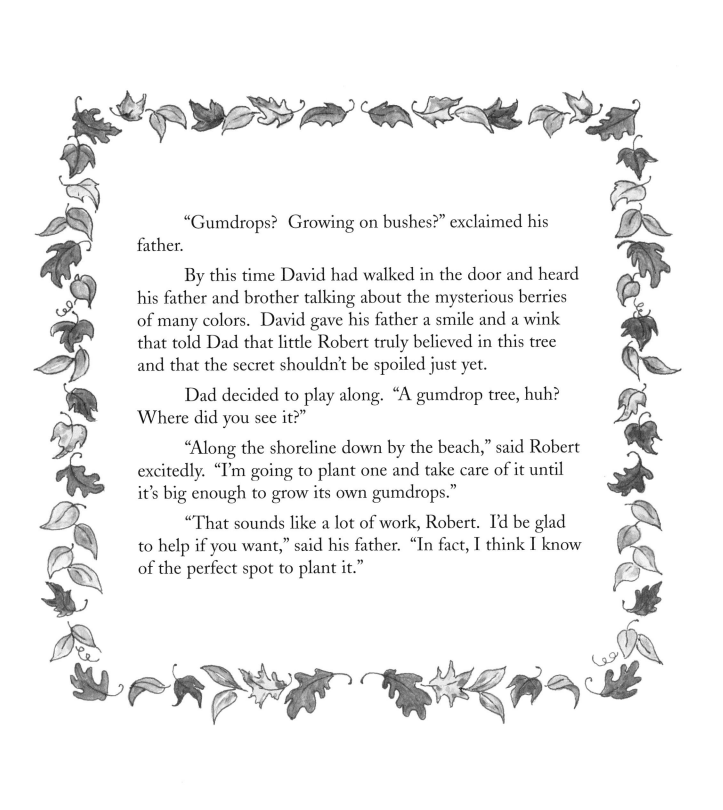

"Gumdrops? Growing on bushes?" exclaimed his father.

By this time David had walked in the door and heard his father and brother talking about the mysterious berries of many colors. David gave his father a smile and a wink that told Dad that little Robert truly believed in this tree and that the secret shouldn't be spoiled just yet.

Dad decided to play along. "A gumdrop tree, huh? Where did you see it?"

"Along the shoreline down by the beach," said Robert excitedly. "I'm going to plant one and take care of it until it's big enough to grow its own gumdrops."

"That sounds like a lot of work, Robert. I'd be glad to help if you want," said his father. "In fact, I think I know of the perfect spot to plant it."

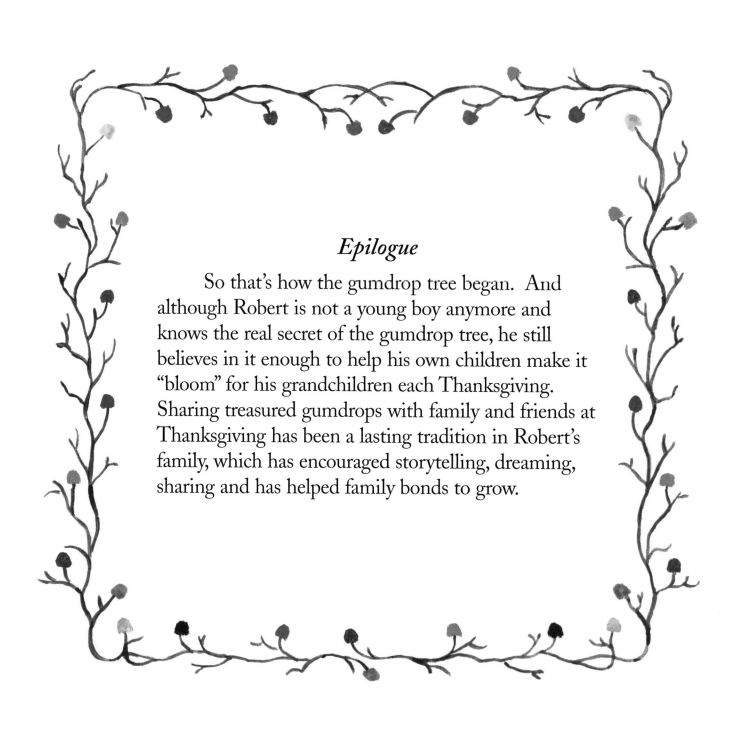

Epilogue

So that's how the gumdrop tree began. And although Robert is not a young boy anymore and knows the real secret of the gumdrop tree, he still believes in it enough to help his own children make it "bloom" for his grandchildren each Thanksgiving. Sharing treasured gumdrops with family and friends at Thanksgiving has been a lasting tradition in Robert's family, which has encouraged storytelling, dreaming, sharing and has helped family bonds to grow.

My Father's Gumdrop Tree Recipe

1 Bush or small tree with low branches
1 16 oz bag of large gumdrops (multi-colored)

With small children out of sight select bush or
small tree with many branches for best effect.
Keep gumdrops at room temperature until ready To
make the bush "bloom" (cold gumdrops won't work!)
Bring clippers to cut tips of little branches. Impale warm
gumdrops on sharp tips of bush. Distribute color to taste.

Printed in the United States
By Bookmasters